THE SPIRIT OF *Liberty*

100 PAINTINGS
by Tsing-fang Chen
for the Centennial Celebration
of
THE STATUE OF LIBERTY
1886–1986
— a special Neo-iconographic series —

「自由女神」百幅連作

陳錦芳

This book is published on the occasion of the Centennial Celebration
of the Statue of Liberty and includes 100 paintings by
T.F. Chen done for the occasion.
Designers: Patricia Mock of Creative Zone, Inc. and T.F. Chen
Typesetting: Skeezo Typography
Printer: Preferred Press, Inc., NYC

First edition.
Published by Lucia Gallery, 90 West Houston St., New York,
N.Y. 10012
Printed in USA

ISBN: 0-9616961-0-9
     0-9616961-1-7 (Deluxe)

THE SPIRIT OF *Liberty*

CHEN 芝

—dedicated to—
My Parents in Heaven
and
Lovers of Liberty
around the World
—T.F. Chen—

Symbol of America

What metaphor shall we use to describe America? Earlier in our history, we spoke of America as a melting pot—a forge in which different cultures, like metals, are transformed by the white heat of freedom to yield an alloy of unprecedented strength.

In recent years, we have talked of the United States as a vivid mosaic of many races, creeds, and ethnic backgrounds. In every city and town of this land we can see not a clash of cultures but each heritage leaving its own imprint and enriching us all.

America is also a kaleidoscope, where the prisms of pluralism continually refract new combinations of cultural genius.

Whatever images we use, the reality continues to be quite astounding. And it would not be so if America were not a country of open doors and open minds.

Where many other countries are founded on fear, our country is founded on freedom.

Where many other societies are torn apart by hate, ours is held together by hope.

In many other countries, an iron curtain descends to block the free flow of people and ideas. In America we refuse to lock people in or lock ideas out.

What better symbol of America's special character is there than the Statue of Liberty, who lights the way to a refuge for the dispossessed, and then frees them to make the most of talents long ignored?

Stephen J. Solarz

Congressman

HON. SIR LEONARD CONNER: Acclaimed "Poet of the Century" by Pope John Paul's "Legion of America" and "The Legion of Mary"; Accorded Golden Laurel Crown as "World Poet Laureate of the Century" by United Poets Laureate International; "Official Poet Laureate" of the (U.S.) "Military Order of the Purple Heart" and (U.S.) Marine Corps Memorial Association; and the U.S.S. Intrepid (permanent Sea, Air & Space Museum at N.Y.C.), as well as other national groups, in addition to innumerable unique awards.

Opus #1,505

"What Is The Lure - of the Lady with the Lamp?"
By The Honorable Sir Leonard Conner

As Premiered by the author at the Beaux Arts Society annual "Spring Festival"
May 3RD, 1986, at the Kitteridge Club, New York City

What is the Lure - of the "Lady with the Lamp." Who stands in New York's harbor day and night,
Her torch - gleaming in the darkness   Radiating serenity - with her Sacred Light?

What ancient muse inspired her creator   And infused her with a spirit that has come to symbolize:
To a hungering mankind: the essence of Freedom   With an aura of dignity - that description defies?

What other mute magnet in the World   Has its Awesome Magic
To infuse Hope and Courage   Into lives - that are nothing less than tragic?

What other silent symbol,   known ev'rywhere on Earth
Holds forth such Priceless Promise,   to Ev'ryone - from birth?

How could this simple statue: A gift from folks in France:
Become a Beacon - for mankind?   Did it happen just by chance?

And when it was erected,   Along America's Eastern shore,
Who could have suspected it would become a symbol   The whole World would adore?

That ev'ry eye that gazed on her   Would shed a tear - despite one's will:
For who could perceive Her Beauty   Without an "electric" thrill!

Yes, for She is literally alive   With a throbbing, pulsing heart,
That draws you to acknowledge Her   In Her own, psychic world apart!

None can resist Her,   No one would even try:
Of all the millions who've beheld Her   She's been the "Apple" of each eye.

So fantastic is Her image,   Such Sheer Joy - just to behold
One could not admire Her more   If She were cast of Solid Gold!

So, what is the Miraculous Secret   Of Her Unparalleled Appeal?
What do the mitered coronet   And flowing robes conceal?

Is it some mesmerizing force: Or, something - Even More:
A Transcendental Power   Like none ever known before?

Emma Lazarus stated it nobly   In her Immortal Poem:
To the world's ... "tired, poor, wretched refuse"...   "Lady Liberty" beckoned All - to a "Home,"

Where None need any longer   Be... "tempest - tossed; yearning - to be Free,"...
But Welcome, as ev'ry Child of God   Has an Inalienable Right to be!

Politicians - may come and go   Indeed, Civilizations may disappear,
But Bartholdi's Blessed Lady, unto Eternity like the Pyramids   Shall Gloriously Stand - right here!

She shall remain an Object of Veneration,   Unto Ev'ry Future Generation:
Until Time Itself is Done,   For the "Lady with the Lamp" - is "Miss America" - Number One! "

*"If I myself felt that spirit here, then
it is certainly here that my statue must
rise; here where people get their first
view of the New World, and where liberty
casts her rays on both worlds."*

Auguste Bartholdi, 1872
Sculptor of the Statue of Liberty

Liberty

*I was astounded and enthralled at my first glimpse of
Dr. T.F. Chen's Statue of Liberty paintings. The beauty,
complexity, and humor of the works delighted me. Even
more, his obvious love and fascination for this great symbol
of America struck me. As an immigrant, Dr. Chen has
viewed Ms. Liberty with a fresh perspective and has helped
the rest of us to see her in all her complexity. It is most
appropriate that the creative energy of an immigrant, one of
the millions who have helped to build America over the last
century, should produce this beautiful gift to the Statue of
Liberty on her centennial.*

*Paul J. Kinney
Museum Curator
The American Museum of Immigration
Statue of Liberty National Monument*

April 29, 1986

FIVE ICONS OF AMERICA

An icon can be any visual image. It can be hallowed—or totally frivolous. Quite fearlessly, Tsing-fang Chen uses every manner of icon, and his iconographic treatments of Liberty are not all deadly serious, any more than America could exist without a sense of humor.

In America, I think, there are only five universal icons: George Washington, Abraham Lincoln, the American flag, Uncle Sam, and the Statue of Liberty.

George Washington is revered as the Father of Our Country. His face, whether on coins or postage stamps, or in a gallery, is instantly recognized. Abraham Lincoln held the Union together and expressed the ultimate worth of people and democratic institutions. He is as instantly recognizable as the First President and arguably even more beloved.

No other human American icons approach either of these.

The most instantly recognized icon of all is the American flag. It is universally recognized throughout the world, but, abroad, it is not universally loved. It stands for the United States of America and for everything anybody wishes to impute to our country, true or not, good or bad. Our flag we love. In some countries there are people who burn it.

Uncle Sam suffers the same fate.

Nobody burns the Statue of Liberty, even in effigy, although there are totalitarian nations which wish they could. Anti-democratic governments have tried to stomp out Liberty, but no one has ever found a way to remove it from the deepest roots of the human soul.

The Statue of Liberty, then, is the most powerful, implacable, and beautiful symbol that America gives to the world. It represents the primordial quality that every living soul, touched by Divinity, yearns for.

This is what Chen has sought to show in his hundred paintings.

—Lawrence Jeppson

Tsing-fang Chen and The Statue of Liberty

LAWRENCE JEPPSON

Let me retell in a few words an ancient Chinese legend. You will smile and nod in recognition of a truth that touches you more deeply than anyone can measure. I will change the legend slightly. Inescapably, you will agree with me that my version is the perfect allegory of our time. Chronicled in Chinese folklore is the tale of a T'ang Dynasty monk who traveled West to study Liberty. He was accompanied by three disciples: a monkey, a white horse, and a pig. The monkey was a fabulous magical creature who could change himself into 72 forms—into smoke, a fly, a tiger, anything. One day he was boasting to Liberty, "I can fly away so fast I can escape from anything."

To prove his brag he flew away abruptly and engraved his name on Five Finger Mountain. But Liberty said to him, "Here is your signature on my palm. It doesn't matter that you can fly. You are always in my power."

The driving desire of all human beings to make choices cannot be taken away; nor can it be ceded successfully. The craving dwells innately within the heart and spirit of man. Whatever our circumstances, as long as we are rational we are all in Liberty's power, forever.

Like the monk of the T'ang dynasty, there is, chronicled in contemporary reality, the adventure of a young Taiwanese artist who also left his homeland to travel West. Like the monk, he found more than he

bargained for. Eventually he discovered an artistic glue—
Neo-Iconography—for binding together the cultures of the world. Like
the monkey, he found himself inescapably in Liberty's hand.

In our allegory, Liberty is personified as the Statue of Liberty, and
Tsing-fang Chen, our latter-day magician, is clearly caught in her hand.
Even though he change himself into 72 forms or a thousand artistic
personna, Chen cannot escape. He does not want to. He has been a
wanderer, in space, in time, and in culture. Just as the statue on Liberty
Island is the perfect icon of Liberty, so Chen is the perfect symbol of all
those who have been drawn to her from a thousand fields and waters.

A naturalized American citizen, Chen loves Liberty. Since the statue
was soon to be a hundred years old, he set out a year ago to paint more
than a hundred tributes to her.

Chen had no thought of aping the woman who sat in the Louvre and
painted more than a thousand replicas of the *Mona Lisa*. The painting of
a stream of maudlin repeats would be as uncreative as counting beads or
spinning prayer wheels. Although a celebrant of Liberty, he had no need
to make empty gestures or do penance. But he did have a need to paint
Liberty in a hundred different ways, calling into service his extraordinary
erudition, his effusive love for all of man's varied expressions of culture
over past millennia, and his passion for the eternal truth of man's
universal freedom-seeking spirit.

Chen's being is filled with an incendiary mix of East and West, of old
and new, of lasting and ephemeral, of material and spiritual . . .
he is a volcano of ideas, ideals, and artistic tools. He is an artist of
mindful passion. In these past few months Chen has created a
commemorative cavalcade to Liberty that has no counterpart, either in
number, variety, inventiveness, or passion, as he shows that Liberty is
bound up inextricably with every human endeavor.

This eye-popping cargo of Liberty litanies is also a hosanna to the
flowering of Neo-Iconography, which is a limitless way of uniting time
and space and esthetic diversity into fresh artistic expressions and insights.
Neo-iconography can make us think, feel, and even laugh.

As the Prophet, Seer, and Agitator for Neo-Iconography, Chen
appropriates visual images from man's treasury of art and experiences and
imaginatively molds them into beautiful and powerful new paintings.
These paintings reward us with fresh thrills and insights without cutting
us off from our visual heritage. As you will see from turning these pages,
he has bound together, in a saturated vision, the cultures of Asia, Europe,
and America to create his astonishing tribute to the Statue of Liberty.

Chen's painting *She Saves* (plate 1) (also known as *Welcome to the
Tempest-Tossed*), which begins this book, is the perfect expression of the
power of freedom and deliverance as symbolized by the Statue of Liberty.

For *She Saves,* Chen has ingeniously adapted part of a very famous

I. Self-portrait, oil on canvas, 20″ × 16″, I-86

painting, Theodore Gericault's *Raft of the Medusa,* to depict the
huddled masses who have come to the United States seeking rescue and a
brighter future.

In the history of art, *Raft of the Medusa* was a watershed painting. First
exhibited in the Salon of 1819, it broke brusquely with the fashions of
Neo-classical art and set currents in motion leading both to Realism and
Romanticism. It is widely considered as being the painting which ushered
in modern art. The story it memorialized was grim, just as have been the
plights of many who have come to our shores.

In 1816 a fleet of four ships set out from Rochefort, France, bound for
Senegal, West Africa, a former colony being returned to France by the
British after Napoleon's Waterloo defeat. The flagship was the
decommissioned warship *Medusa* carrying 405 people. The expedition
was badly led; even the captain was a political hack, and his decisions
were soon manipulated by others of the entourage who knew even less
about the sea. The ships went separate ways, and the *Medusa* ran
aground on an Atlantic sandbar of the Arguin Banks about forty miles
off the Sahara coast. More than half the people took to small boats, most
of them overloaded, except for the two boats carrying the captain and the
new governor and his family, which were much underloaded, leaving 150
low-rank officers, engineers, soldiers, and commercial people to fend for
themselves on a jerry-built raft which was so overburdened that it floated

below the water surface. By the time the raft was accidentally found by rescue ship thirteen days later, only 15 men survived. The others had been swept off by high seas, died of hunger and thirst, or perished combatting one another.

The tragedy created a major scandal. In preparation for his monumental work, which now hangs in the Louvre, Gericault interviewed survivors and actually constructed a replica of part of the raft. He memorialized the moment when the survivors sighted a rescue speck, the shallow-draft *Argus,* which probably had not yet spotted them.

Chen changes the virtually unseeable *Argus* to the prominent Statue of Liberty with her torch held high. He does not use all of the *Raft of the Medusa* but takes for his icon only the right half of the painting, with its optimistic pyramidal structuring. Nor does he counterfeit Gericault's technique or palette, for those things are immaterial to Chen's purposes. In fact, the Gericault palette of dark foreboding would be contrary to Chen's objective. Instead he has transformed the surface into the much more optimistic feeling of Seurat's Pointillism. The variety of colors that this entails better symbolizes the unending variety of the millions who have found rescue on American shores.

The people in the painting are ragtag, and some who set out have died, but those who have survived are about to enter a promised land.

One of the most urbane and well-informed artists of the nineteenth century, Jean Francois Millet (1814–1875) did not immediately find public favor, especially with the French middle class, who viewed his canvases, which glorified the moral superiority of hard labor, as revolutionary. While the French were ignoring him, Millet found an appreciative audience in the United States, where the Puritan ideal of work was a fundamental part of the national mystique. American collectors like Quincy Adams Shaw, William H. Vanderbilt, J.P. Morgan, Mrs. Potter Palmer, and John G. Johnson brought French peasants to America as immortalized images on canvas.

Chen sees a deep linkage between Liberty and religious expression. In *Praying in the New Land* (plate 2) he takes two peasant figures from Millet's *Angelus* (1859), which is named after the Latin prayer recited at the start of day, noon, and end of day. There is a monumental dignity to these two icons which harmonizes nicely with the silhouetted statue and the bright sun behind it. As with *She Saves,* Chen has stripped away unnecessary details from the original image and changed the style from Barbizon to Post-Impressionist Pointillism. It is a quite appropriate alteration, since Seurat was considerably influenced by Millet. More importantly, the new colors mean new lands, new opportunity, new freedoms grounded in everlasting principles of work and decency.

Modifying these same two Millet icons even more, Chen makes quite a different version of *Praying in the New Land* (plate 3). He has made the figures more stark, less European, more universal, but in counterplay to these changes he has added a hotter, less amenable land and a digging fork, a vegetable basket, and a wheelbarrow. Tiny twin towers of the World Trade Center in the distance accentuate the greater power of the statue. The image is completed by ultrasonic jets cutting the corners.

City Gleaners (plate 9) is a devastating commentary. Chen freely uses three peasants from another Millet, the familiar *Gleaners* (1857). Although the colors and tonal placements of the painting are lovely, these ladies have not chanted the Angelus, nor does their work seem so ennobling. They are picking up the trash of a profligate society, scavenging cans from a dump. The figure on the right carries a totebag imprinted I LOVE NEW YORK. Do they scavenge the soft drink cans to clean up the mess of litterers, or are they gleaning to have something to sell? Take your choice. The image of Liberty standing on a Classic Coke can is delicious. Chen is not without considerable humor.

Another favorite of mine is *Contemplating Liberty* (plate 4), perhaps because the subjects of George Caleb Bingham (1811–1871) are so quintessentially American. *Fur Traders Descending the Missouri* (1845) gives us icons of the wanderers and rough, pioneering subduers of the Trans-Mississippi West. Chen has marvelously mixed up time and place in this laud to Liberty. He has snitched the fur traders from the calm isolation of the primitive Missouri River to the metropolitan harbor of New York City and today's skyline. To accentuate the contrast he has added a tall ship and another sailing vessel.

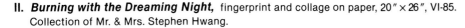
II. ***Burning with the Dreaming Night,*** fingerprint and collage on paper, 20″ × 26″, VI-85. Collection of Mr. & Mrs. Stephen Hwang.

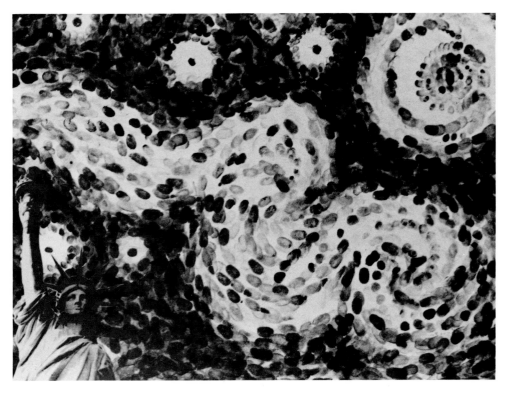

A second version of this painting, *From the Missouri to the Hudson* (plate 5) simplifies the painted surface, eliminating the multicolors of Pointillism to broad, flat, and powerful silhouettes, a cleansed art of contemporary America.

Another quintessential American piece is *Sunday Morning, Liberty!* (plate 7), which takes a popular image from Edward Hopper (1882–1967), *Early Sunday Morning* (1930). Caleb Bingham represents wild, unpopulated Mid-America of the early nineteenth century, but Hopper symbolizes stark, seedy urban America of a century later. In either aspect of American culture and history, the situation is what it is because of a matrix of choices made by many. Chen's introduction of the Liberty icon in such a dramatic fashion in the Hopper picture drives home the point that even when no human beings are in view, the social context is a product of human decisions.

Chen's life is full of heroes. His selection of icons to go with Liberty reveals these deep admirations. Among his heroes are other painters, and when he serves us their images as part of the philosophical and esthetic point he is making, he is saluting these heroes.

Henri Matisse is a frequent hero. In *Five Races in Harmony*, a marvelous piece of Neo-Iconography from 1976, our Bicentennial year, Chen painted each of the figures from Matisse's *The Dance* a different color, and he put a gold-hued Matisse in the center of the circle. This dramatic interpretation simultaneously expressed his admiration for Matisse and demonstrated his own overpowering faith in the coming together of men in one closer family. In *United Around Liberty Lady* (plate 16) he has repeated the racial coloring he gave the dancers, but even though he has replaced Matisse with a blue Statue of Liberty, the homage to Matisse is undiminished.

Chen's affection for Chagall is manifest in *Chagall Visiting the Statue of Liberty* (plate 21); *I love Paris, I love Liberty* (plate 22); and *Violin Duet for Liberty* (plates 19, 20). Ms. Bain-Smith's commentaries on these pieces need no elaboration here.

Other immediately recognized artists include Kandinsky, Van Gogh, Klee, Miro, Leger, Degas, Giacometti, Bonnard, Picasso, Braque, Monet, Mondrian, Hokusai, Hiroshige, and Winslow Homer.

Several of these homages offer radical revisions of Liberty's Auguste Bartholdi image, and when they do the results can be funny and charming. One of my favorites is *Paul Klee's Guardian of Liberty* (plate 46). Everything is changed. The Lady has become a sailor and the torch a flaming hand-held staff that rises from the ground. The island looks like a floating tub, as if the guardian could circumnavigate Manhattan, protecting the citizens from seademons while calling everyone to play.

I laughed when I saw *Seurat's Statue of Liberty* (plate 43) and the *Awakening Gypsy* (plate 49). In the former Chen has taken a single bustled lady from *Sunday Afternoon on the Island of la Grande Jatte*,

III. *Seurat's Liberty Lady,* charcoal and conte on paper, 26" × 20", VIII-85

given her the torch, and put her on a pedestal which actually is the stovepipe hat of her companion. The painting is full of fun, but it does not make fun. The other painting borrows a Henri Rousseau Gypsy and, with the humor, gives her dignity and power. The moon is a Chen icon for the spiritual insight of the East.

The East (meeting West, frequently) is manifest in several pieces, although not as often as I would have expected, knowing Chen's previous work. *Greetings from the East* (plate 24) is filled with Buddhist icons, from a sky composed of Tibetan floor frescoes to the diadem inserts around the Lady's crown. The latter are repeated with even more telling effect, and with wry manipulation, in *Nesting Blessings* (plate 25).

More dramatic is *Rising Tides of Liberty* (plate 94), which takes Hokusai's *Great Wave of Kanagawa* and replaces its view of Mount Fuji with Liberty and the New York skyline. Chen sees the wave as the universal tide of freedom, and in this context the painting rivals *She Saves,* which begins this book. A lovelier piece however, is *Gracious Rain of Liberty* (plate 91), with its graceful wood bridge from a Hiroshige print dominating the foreground.

(continued on page 82)

"Give me your tired, your poor,
Your huddled masses yearning to breathe free,
The wretched refuse of your teeming shore,
Send these, the homeless tempest-tossed to me,
I lift my lamp beside the golden door!"

Emma Lazarus (1849-1887)

1. *She Saves* (or ***Welcome to the Tempest-Tossed***)
oil on canvas, 60″ × 40″, XII-85
source: T. Gericault, *The Raft of the Medusa*,
1819, Louvre, Paris

2. **Praying in the New Land (I),** oil on canvas, 24″ × 30″, XII-85,
collection of Dr. & Mrs. Tzeu-shong and May-sing Yang,   source: J.F. Millet, *Angelus,* 1867.

"Their tasks
completed in France.
Millet's peasants,
transplanted,
pray in America.
The Sun, the universal light
silhouettes
their new shrine,
the Liberty Lady.

Peace will come."

Priscella Bain-Smith.

3. **Praying in the New Land (II),** paintstik on canvas, 30″ × 40″, XII-85

4. *Contemplating Liberty,* oil on canvas, 30″ × 40″, XII-85,

source: G.C. Bingham (1811–1879), *Fur Traders Descending the Missouri,* 1845, The Metropolitan Museum of Modern Art, NY

5. *From the Missouri to the Hudson,* paintstik on canvas, 30″ × 40″, XII-85

6. **Sailing in Liberty,** oil on canvas, 36″ × 48″, III-86,   source: Winslow Homer (1836–1910) *Breezing Up,* 1876, National Gallery of Art, Washington, D.C.

American Lady

"Lady in harbor

American lady,
Alone, she stands
And gazes, proudly,
Welcoming visitors;
Her lifted arm of strength
Light of liberty and oceans and land.

She holds the gift of time,
And the blessing—
Freedom's longest, finest hour."

Edward Patrick McCue

"Quietly, in harmony with the stillness
of a Hopper morning, Chen's statue
proclaims her universality.
Those inside soon will waken to her
message."

P.B-S.

7. **Sunday Morning, Liberty!**
oil on canvas, 60″ × 40″, I-86
source: Edward Hopper, *Early Sunday Morning,* 1930
Whitney Museum of American Art

8. *I Lift My Lamp beside the Golden Door,* paintstik on paper, 29.5" × 41.5", 5-XII-85

*"The Lady stands
proud and erect.
The torch of Liberty
held high in her hand.
A symbol to the world:
an embodiment of freedom,
peace and justice*

*City gleaners behind;
humble and slouched
The empty soda cans gripped
in brown, wrinkled hands.
An embodiment of hard work and truth;
the pedestal from which
the Lady stands."*

Kathy Lee

9. *City Gleaners,*
acrylic on canvas, 72" × 50", XII-85
collection of Mr. and Mrs. Paul and Mary Lee
sources: J.F. Millet, *The Gleaners,* 1857,
Louvre, Paris
Paul Gauguin, *And the Gold of their Bodies,* 1901
Musee du Jeu de Paume, Paris

CHEN 荃
9-1-86

13. *The Burning Passion,* oil on foamcore, 20″ × 8″, I-86

"The sacrifice of your loved ones
has stirred the soul of our nation
and, through the pain, our hearts
have been opened to a profound truth:
the future is not free, the story
of all human progress is one of a
struggle against all odds. We learn
again that this America, which
Abraham Lincoln called the last
best hope of man on Earth, was built
on heroism and noble sacrifice. It
was built by men and women like our
seven star voyagers, who answered
a call beyond duty, who gave more
than was expected or required, and
who gave it with little thought to
worldly reward.

. . . .

Today, the frontier is space and
the boundaries of human knowledge.
Sometimes, when we reach for the
stars, we fall short. But we must
pick ourselves up again and press
on despite the pain. Our nation is
indeed fortunate that we can still draw
on our immense reservoirs of courage,
character and fortitude — and that we are
still blessed with heros like those of
the space shuttle Challenger.

—excerpt from President Reagan's
eulogy at a memorial service for
the seven Challenger astronauts
at the Johnson Space Center in
Houston on January 31st, 1986

14. *Challenging Free Frontiers*
acrylic and spray on canvas
72″ × 50″, 31-I-86

18. ***Blessing the Torch,*** oil pastel on paper, 20″ × 26″, 23-VI-85,   source: Botticelli, *Birth of Venus,* 1486, Uffizi, Florence

"Above the peopled beach,
Boticellian zephyrs bless
the Torch. They've come far
in time and space for this event.
And soon they will
rejoin the ship below
in perfect harmony."

P.B.-S.

"So many flags; so much freedom.
Rousseau's skybound and winged
Liberty Lady trumpet
invitations to our Lady. The French boats come . . .
the Liberty Birds come . . .
even the men from Mount Rushmore come.
The torch is too significant to ignore."

P.B.-S.

17. ***Hail to the Statue of Liberty,***
    acrylic on canvas, 72″ × 50″, V85
    sources: H., Rousseau, *Liberty's Invitation to the artists to Take Part*
        in the 22nd Exhibit of the Independents, 1906;
        I Myself, Portrait-Landscape, 1890

19. *Violin Duet for Liberty,*
oil on canvas, 60″ × 46″, XI-85 to III-86
sources: Chagall, *The Fiddler,* 1912–13, Amsterdam, Stedelijk Museum
The Green Violinist, 1918, Solomon R. Guggenheim Museum

*"Their music never stops.
Chagall's Fiddlers fiddle
and Chen's Statue becomes
a performing platform
for their universal notes.
With Chen, Harmony dominates
and Our lady remains silent
yet strong."*

P.B.-S.

20. *Violin Duet for Liberty (II),*
mixed media on paper, 26″ × 20″, IX-85
collection of Dr. & Mrs. Ming-Liang and
Ya-hwei Lee

*"Chagall's couples float
idyllically over villages,
over countryside, over
other couples. They know
and rejoice in the message
of Chen's Statue: there can
never be too much freedom."*

P.B.-S.

21. *Chagall Visiting the Statue of Liberty,*
acrylic on canvas, 72″ × 50″, IV-85
sources: Chagall, *Over the Town,* 1917–1918,
Tretyerkov Gallery, Moscow
The Birthday, 1915–23,
Solomon R. Guggenheim Museum

41. *Burning in Cosmic Rhythm,* mixed media on paper, 40″ × 52″, X-85.

(overleaf)
*"Leger, conscience of plights of the working peoples,
now becomes the perfect platform for a new image of
Our Lady. Although unclassical, She now is just as
magnificent. Her crown, leaves, so attractive that
birds fly quickly to her; her torch so vibrant that
clouds reflect the intensity. Leger's Lady is powerful,
pliant, and peaceful."*

P.B.-S.

(overleaf)
42. *Leger's Statue of Liberty,*
mixed media on boardpaper,
43″ × 27″, 16-VI-85
source: Leger, *Self-Portrait,* c. 1937, Paris.

44. *Miro's Magic Lady,* mixed media on paper, 26″ × 20″, 14-VI-85.

45. *Degas's Statue of Liberty,* oil pastel on paper, 26″ × 20″, XII-85, source: Degas, *End of an Arabesque,* 1877, Musee du Jeu de Paume.

(preceding page)
43. *Seurat's Statue of Liberty,* oil on canvas, 48″ × 36″, VIII-85.
   collection of Mme Frances Pecker, NY,
     source: G. Seurat, *Sunday Afternoon on La Grande Jatte,* 1886,
      Art Institute, Chicago.

*"Boats pass calmly; behind, the Twin Towers
stand almost not noticing the subtle change
of icons. Seurat's Lady now our Statue of Liberty.
Her base, a high top hat as dignified and sturdy
as her own posture. All echo the powerful message
of Chen's universality: male and female; natural
and manmade environments; cultures proudly
combining with cultures."*

       P.B.-S.

*"Chen sees the secure New York
with Klee and watches the Liberty
Sailor subtly balance the precarious
Freedom by keeping the disrupting
denizens in eternal limbo."*

       P.B.-S.

46. *Paul Klee's Guardian of Liberty*
paintstik on canvas, 72″ × 50″, XI-85,
source: Klee, *Battle Scene from the
Fantastic Comic Opera: Sinbad the Sailor,* 1923.

47. *African Statue of Liberty (I),* mixed media on paper, 26″ × 20″, VII-85.

*"It's African.
It's American.
Once more it's Chen
combining cultures.
She's powerful no matter
where she is.
Bags of spirits
no longer useful
slip sluggishly
from her body.
The torch and flame
triumphant!"*

P.B.-S.

48. *African Statue of Liberty (II),* mixed media on paper, 26″ × 20″, VII-85.

"Proudly Rousseau's Gypsy
awakens and hoists high
her torch of Freedom.
The lion, now innocuous,
remains in the past
as does the Moon.
She, instead, ⌐ ⌐p
her carpeted valise
with guitar and staff
faces a new destiny —
which in Chen's world
can only be positive."

P.B.-S.

49. The Awakening Gypsy,
acrylic on canvas,
66″ × 32″, VII-85.
source: H. Rousseau,
The Sleeping Gypsy, 1897
Museum of Modern Art, NY

58. *Picasso's Torch (I),* acrylic and spray on canvas, 36″ × 48″, V-85,   source: Picasso, *Guernica,* 1937

59. *Picasso's Torch (II),* Indian ink on paper, 20″ × 26″, V-85.

60. *Playing with Big Apples,* color pencil on paper, 26″ × 20″, 23-XI-86,   source: Picasso, *Bather with a Ball,* 1932.

63. *Liberty Lady at the Beach,* charcoal and color pencil on paper, 29.5″ × 41.5″, 12-XI-85
sources: Renoir, *Blond Bather,* 1905, oil; Picasso, *Bathers.* 1918, Biarritz, oil.

"Seemingly unnoticed, She rests
and bathes along the beach with
those She's been protecting.
Her crown and torch placed
tenderly beside her. From these
unexpected precious moments,
She will regain her strength
and begin steadfastly the next
100 year vigil."

P.B.-S.

"Playfully and gleefully,
but also seriously, Art and
Liberty combine their energies.
They need each other. Chen's
Liberty Lady struggles to keep
the Torch upright as Art struggles
to put inspiration into her
mouth and mind. The Moon and
Manhattan wait quietly outside
knowing all will be fair
in the future."

P.B.-S.

62. *Liberty, Mother of Peace and Art,*
charcoal and Indian ink on paper,
collection of Professor & Mrs. Ching-lai Hwang
41.5″ × 29.5″, XI-85.
source: Picasso, *Mother and Child,* 1921 or 22, oil

64. *Bathing Under the Light of Liberty,* oil on canvas, 48″ × 56″, I-86.
source: Cezanne, *Large Bathers,* 1899–1905, Philadelphia Museum of Art.

65. *Bathing Under the Light of Liberty (II),* paintstick on paper, 20″ × 26″, I-86.

67. *Burning High,* acrylic on canvas, 60″ × 30″, VIII-85.
source: Miro, *Dog Barking at the Moon,* 1926,
Philadelphia Museum of Art.

66. *Surrealist Liberty,* oil and collage on canvas, 40″ × 30″, I-86.
source: G. de Chirico, *Premonitory Portrait of William Apollinaire,* 1914, Paris.

68. *Crescent Liberty,* paintstik on paper, 24″ × 19″, 19-VII-85.

69. *Firework for Liberty,* mixed media on paper, 26″ × 20″, 4-VII-85.

70. *Liberty Lady in Fashion,* mixed media on paper, 26″ × 20″, 24-VI-85.

71. *Growing with the Twin Towers,* paintstik on paper, 26″ × 20″, VIII-85.

72. *Watch out the Fire, New Yorker,* crayon on paper, 26″ × 20″, 6-VII-85.

73. *Remembering de Kooning,*
mixed media on paper, 38″ × 25″, 16-XII-85.

74. *Liberty on Wall,* mixed media on paper,
38″ × 25″, 16-XII-85.

75. *Paris Wall or New York Wall?,* mixed media on paper,
38″ × 25″, 17-XII-85.

76. *Beacon, Day and Night,* mixed media on paper, 26″ × 40″, X-85.

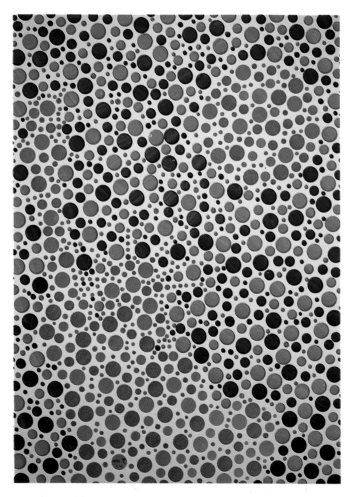

77. *Seeing or not Seeing,*
magic marker on paper,
41.5″ × 29.5″, I-86.

78. *Liberty in Cubism (I),* oil pastel on paper, 26″ × 20″, II-86.

79. *Liberty in Cubism (II),* oil pastel on paper, 26″ × 20″, II-86.

80. *Liberty in Cubism (III),*
oil pastel on paper, 26″ × 20″, II-86;
78. 79. 80. collection of
Dr. & Mrs. Michael H. Shiau.

81. *Liberty to Victory (I),* acrylic on canvas, 40″ × 30″, II-86.　　　**82.** *Liberty to Victory (II),* acrylic on canvas, 40″ × 30″, II-86.

83. *I Need You,* oil and collage on canvas, 40″ × 30″, II-86.

84. *Liberty Lady (I),* acrylic on canvas, 40″ × 30″, II-86.

85. *Liberty Lady (II),* acrylic on canvas, 40″ × 30″, II-86.

86. *Liberty Lady (III),* acrylic on canvas, 40″ × 30″, II-86.

87. *Jeanne d'Arc of Our Time,* acrylic on canvas, 48″ × 36″, XI-85

88. *Fire Bird,* paintstik on paper, 20″ × 26″, II-86.

89. *Fire from Heaven,* paintstik on paper, 26″ × 20″, II-86.

90. *Liberty Nature,* mixed media on paper, 26″ × 20″, III-86.

"It's raining,
but it doesn't matter.
It is a gracious rain.
Hiroshige's workers
still go to work;
Hiroshige's workers
still return from work.
Boats in the river
work and play;
Chen's Statue
looms gigantically
near the Eastern Bridge
connecting itself
to the Western metropolis.
The East-West Convergency
nears completion."

P.B.-S.

91. *Gracious Rain of Liberty,*
acrylic on canvas, 66″ × 44″, II-86.
source: Hiroshige, *Ohasi Bridge
and Atake in Sudden Shower*
from the series *100 Views of
Famous Places in Edo,* 1857.

92. *Welcoming Water Lillies,*
acrylic on canvas, 36″ × 48″, II-86,
source: Monet, *Water Lilies,* c. 1920, oil,
Musee Marmottan, Paris.

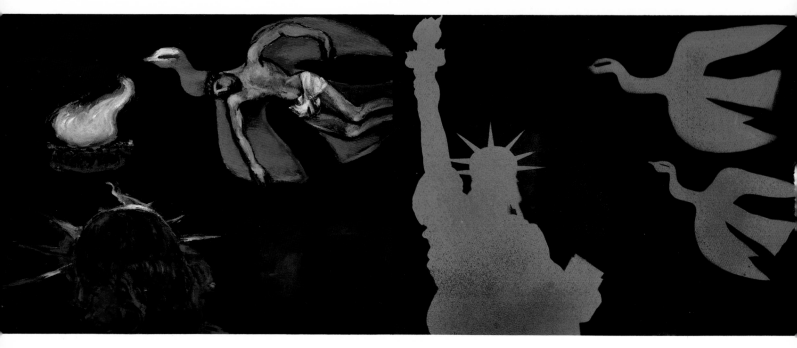

93. *To Freedom, to Light, to Sacrifice, to Saintity,* acrylic and spray on canvas, 36″ × 192″, VI-85 to III-86 (right to left).
sources: G. Braque, *Birds,* 1956, *The Bird and His Nest,* Paris.
Van der Weyden, *Descent from the Cross,* 15th century, Prado, Madrid.

94. *Rising Tide of Liberty,* mixed media on canvas, 50″ × 72″, V-85,
source: Hokusai, *Great Wave off Kanagawa, #4, The 36 Views of Mount Fuji.*

*"Greet the Universal Tide of Freedom.
Meet Chen's universal boat people
drifting from many lands, from many
times, to this Icon of Peace. These
are the unfortunates of the world
and the Liberty Lady hoists high
her torch to welcome them."*

P.B.-S.

Soaring Like Birds

"Over your head the vast expanse of sky
under your feet, a great wonderful Land
to the distant shore your light is casting

Were it not for that sort of voice, color, and feeling
you would remain unknown, even one thousand years passed by

Upright erected, you command the bay
casting your hope upon people's Mind

You are the torchlight for seafaring tribes
reaching out your voice to all mankind

Man demands Dignity, Quality, Humanity
forever enduring as Our dreams

Soaring like birds
swimming like fishes
moving like animals

radiating like God, your ultimate brightness
silently, unceasingly

bringing Liberty, Peace, and Love
to every corner of the Earth."

Lin Jong-teh
11 March 1986

96. *Liberty Bird in Flight,*
mixed media on paper, 28″ × 22″, VI-85,
collection of Mr. & Mrs. Paul & Mary Lee.

Tsing-fang Chen and the Statue of Liberty
(continued from page 15)

A *style* of painting can also be an icon, as in *The Burning Passion* (plate 13), the four different silhouettes of plate 55, *Seeing or Not Seeing* (plate 77, inspired by a magazine ad campaign), *Liberty on Wall* (plate 74), *Remembering de Kooning* (plate 73), *Computerizing Liberty* (plate 53), *Liberty in Cubism* (plate 78–80), and others.

Like many of the men and women represented by *She Saves (Welcome to the Tempest-Tossed)*, Chen was a wanderer who felt barred from his native land because of constraints on civil liberties.

Tsing-fang Chen was born to a humble family in the village of Kueizen on the south of Taiwan (Formosa) in 1936. Taiwan was Japanese until the end of the Second World War. The Japanese were eager to catch up with the West, and they grafted to Formosa many Western influences.

As an infant, Chen loved to paw through books depicting the ferocious exploits of Japanese samurai. At two and three he was drawing on walls with chalk and scratching designs on the earth. In elementary school he was the best pupil in drawing.

There are two strong influences in Oriental painting. Best known to the West is painting with brush and ink, the calligraphic art of the literati and mandarins. The other school is popular art, the stuff of everyday existence. Taiwanese are not mandarins. They are workers, hard workers, and they live in a religious atmosphere of mixed Buddhism, Taoism, Confucianism, and a little Christianity. Their landscape is chockablock with temples, and every square foot of surface, round or flat, is decorated with flowers, dramatic figures, folk heroes, calligraphy, symbols. This was Chen's heritage.

Chen's view was permanently marked by the color that surrounded him. Southern Taiwan is a tropical land dominated by hot reds and oranges. All the houses in his village were made with red brick and different tones of red rooftiles. In the hot tropical sun the roofs became blinding fire. Contrasting were the strong greens of the jungle and the rich blues of ocean and sky.

When Chen left grade school at fourteen for a stiff high school in Tainan, he was torn away from these natural influences by the Westernized curriculum.

The next year he encountered a Sunday painter, Vincent Hwang, who owned fifty art books purchased in Japan. Chen devoured the books—and was in turn devoured by Van Gogh, Blue and Rose Picasso, Matisse, Miro, Utrillo, and the Post-Impressionists.

The next year Chen became a student of Chang Ch'ang-hua, an excellent painter who taught him the methods of Cezanne and how to catch volume, proportion, and movement in the French way of the *Ecole des Beaux Arts*. He spent every available hour in the studio. Typically, from a plaster cast Chen sketched the head of the *Venus de Milo* more than three hundred times.

Meanwhile, Chen discovered an enormous body of Chinese popular literature—historical novels from the mainland—and the next year made another discovery which turned him upside down: Shakespeare, Gorky, Hugo, Balzac, Cervantes, Shelley, Byron, Heine, Lamartine, and especially Goethe.

Every day he heard a noontime concert of classical Western music. Painting, literature, and music kept him in a perpetual state of emotional bubbling, and his brain and heart filled at an enormous rate.

Chen became one of the few exceptionally qualified students admitted to National Taiwan University without undergoing competitive examinations.

He had to major in French literature because the university lacked an art curriculum. He wanted to try for a scholarship to study art in France but after graduation had to fulfill his year of compulsory military service.

The Moral Rearmament Movement was looking for fifty young Chinese for an international tour expected to go to former French and Belgian colonies in Africa. Chen and a friend were accepted, but their path suddenly went elsewhere—to Japan, India, Switzerland, Germany, Sweden, and Norway...and then to America for a four-month swing through Michigan, Louisiana, Oklahoma, Texas, and Illinois.

Although he did not actually see the Statue of Liberty on this trip, he knew of her and felt her torch.

For eleven months Chen filled sketchbooks and met notable people. The atmosphere was new, disciplined, visionary, committed, religious, productive, idealistic. Meetings made use of local cultural resources of all kinds, and Chen was nourished in unexpected ways.

Chen says of this experience, "From this ideal to rebuild the world I saw I had a universal religion, the family of humanity. I joined the family of all races to rebuild the world. I regard the world as one, with people mixed together to influence each other. That type of life inspires me. An artist can use his art as a tool to rebuild the world."

Chen's credo was fixed. His artistic vision, however, was still in infancy.

His most excruciating dilemmas still lay ahead . . . dilemmas which impinged inescapably on principles of Liberty.

In 1963, soon after returning to Taiwan, he received his fellowship to France, where he was destined to remain for twelve years.

In Paris Chen jumped simultaneously into two fulltime careers. He pursued an academic path which lead to a Ph.D. in art history from the Sorbonne and a painter's path with years of study at the *Ecole Nationale Superieure des Beaux Arts.* His painter's life was notable for a sweep of exhibitions in France, Germany, Belgium, Italy, and—in absentia—Taiwan.

He wrote extensively about the European art scene for Taiwanese periodicals, published three books on art in Chinese, and translated St. Exupery.

But his life was not smooth.

The supercharged stimulation of Paris was overwhelming. A transplant between opposite cultures, Chen was beset by an overwhelming identity crisis, a crisis which had been building geometrically since he entered his first Japanese-influenced grade school.

He faced conflicts of language, race, culture, politics, philosophy, religion, art, art roots, aspirations, interests, personality . . .

For twelve years Tsing-fang Chen lived, painted, and exhibited in Paris. Ultimately his productive work went through four steps before he found his shattering—or rather his binding— answer.

First he was a Post-Impressionist.

Then for a very short time he was a Fauve. The Fauve palette was a natural extension of the color influences of Southern Taiwan.

From 1968–1970 he re-discovered the East and took up an abstract simulation of archaic Chinese characters. He was in the same groove as Zao Wou-ki, Hans Hartung, and Pierre Soulages.

Sensing new ties with Taiwan, he launched an outpouring of Formosan folklore. The subject matter actually had more ancient Chinese roots, often from the Han and the T'ang dynasties. His paintings were original and full of power.

"It was the orthodox living art," he explains,. "but I couldn't stay on that theme. I was not living in that society."

Then came Chen's fifth level—an explosion! Neo-Iconography!

It came as a climax of a natural evolution that integrated a whole lot more than his four earlier levels. It seemed to strike as a series of brilliant, close-together flashes.

Intellectual nuclear fusions!

Chen explains. "It was difficult now for a painter to have his own image. It is difficult to establish a new style. Everything seems to have been tried. I solved the problem through philosophy."

I coined the term Neo-Iconography in 1978 to describe what Chen had invented. *In its simplest terms,* as I wrote, *Neo-Iconography is based upon the creative manipulation of recognized images. Art and society are*

IV. *Liberty and Justice,* charcoal on paper, 41.5″ × 21.5″, XI-85, collection of Mme. C. Dawn.

held together by a matrix of shared visual experiences. Within these shared images is preserved our sense of history and cultural reality. Anything the eye can see is an image, and every image can be an icon, that is, an image with symbolical meaning.

Dr. Chen, then, is the prophet of Neo-Iconography, a new art which draws in marvelous ways from old art and the current art and from every symbol flashing in the consciousness of man. He is an exciting matchmaker of West and East. He is the innovator of an artistic renaissance that, by using our visual images with mix-and-match cunning, seeks to bind together a confused and fragmented world.

Never lacking energy, Chen also became the Secretary General of the World Federation of Formosan Clubs. His duties took him to almost every big city in Europe, America, and Japan, but never to Taiwan. The clubs' objectives were cultural, but he also associated with expatriates who actively called for greater political freedom in Taiwan. He moved to America in 1975, living first in New York, then in Washington, D.C., and finally in New York again. Chen became an American citizen in 1983, and in 1984 visited his native land and exhibited his art.

Caught in Liberty's hand, Chen has elected to reveal her through Neo-Iconography. Even though he has painted her portrait in a hundred different ways, his reservoir of visions is far from emptied, and he could paint a hundred more and never exhaust his cultural quarry. Although the centennial was the peg, he has painted her because he is one of the tens of millions of immigrants who have come to American shores for the freedoms she exemplifies. As a naturalized Amerian citizen, Dr. Chen is a witness to all the blessings represented by the lady.

He has painted her portraits also because she represents the psychic crux of billions of other people who remain in their native lands, whatever the culture or the political system.

Depending upon your views of art, many of these portraits may seem unconventional. Their variety, as well as their power, simply underscores the many faces Liberty allows us all to enjoy. ▮

Mr. & Mrs. Lawrence Jeppson visiting Chen's exhibit.

About the author:

Lawrence Jeppson: curator, international art consultant, writer, is America's foremost authority on contemporary Aubusson tapestries and is the founder of AcroEditions, publishers of fine, multiple-original art. During the past 30 years, he has organized and supported hundreds of museum and gallery exhibitions, written extensively about art, lectured and served as advisor to institutional and private collectors. He was editor and publisher of *Contemporary Art Reports* and wrote a syndicated newspaper column, "Moments in Art."

His published books include:
Un Coup d'Oeil Honnete sur Les Mormons. Paris, 1951
Murals of Wool, Washington, 1960
The Fabulous Frauds: Fascinating Tales of Great Art Forgeries, New York, 1970; London, 1971.
The Neo-Iconography of Tsing-fang Chen, Washington, 1978
Twelve Encounters with George Andreas. Washington, 1984

Preparation of *William Henry Clapp, the Gentle Impressionist* is nearly finished, and publication of three novels is expected shortly: *The Voice from the Mountain,* an international thriller of art authentication, rape, murder, and espionage set shortly after the 1968 Russian takeover of Czechoslovakia; *But the Devil Was There,* the tale of a young printmaker, an old, semi-mad master painter, and a Cherokee minister set in Philadelphia in 1842; and *Eva Kiss,* the Hollywood adventure of a beautiful Hungarian countesse and refugee from the 1956 suppression who discovers extraordinary powers of the occult—and uses them!

Why "100"?   by T.F. Chen

During the spring of 1985, a strong desire came to me that I would paint 100 paintings about the Statue of Liberty for Her Centennial Birthday. A rare occasion for me indeed. Not only am I an naturalized American, an immigrant to whom the Statue of Liberty has been for decades "the Mother of Exiles," but also in many ways, like Our Liberty Lady, I combine Paris and New York, France and the United States.

Granted a scholarship by the French government, I left Taiwan in 1963 and stayed in Paris for twelve years, earned a Ph.D. in art history from La Sorbonne, and spent seven years at L'Ecole Nationale Superieure des Beaux Arts in Paris. Quite naturally, France became my second homeland. Born in Paris, the Statue of Liberty was presented as a gift of the French people to the American people. She brought from Europe the light of enlightenment: Liberty, Equality and Fraternity to this new land where hope and opportunity stretch wide their arms. Time passed. She saw the First World War and welcomed the soldiers of the Second World War coming home from Europe. Besides Freedom, She symbolizes Victory and Peace. Now, more than just one of the symbols for America, She is a beloved universal "Icon."

An icon is a cultural image with symbolic meaning. An apple, a flower, a man, all are natural images. But the Big Apple, Van Gogh's sunflower, and an astronaut can become icons. Among innumerable monumental sculptures, the Statue of Liberty is an icon, an "Icon" with a big "I". In our age of image and media, icons stand out as crystalized concepts for our thinking and feeling. In art, icon becomes more and more the starting point of creation; especially in my personal art style (named "Neo-iconography" by Lawrence Jeppson ten years ago), icon is the subject, the content, and the message of my creation. Through icon, time and space, history and cultures can be "glued" together, to express, to surprise, to tell, to imagine, to dream, to discover, to cover, to sophisticate, to philosophize, to tease, to please, to preach, to teach, to moralize, to humanize, even to "humorize" . . . in short, to create, at your will, a new world, a new history, a new culture, may I say, a new universal culture of the fifth dimension, combining time, space, and conscience.

Recent photo of Chen's family.
On the wall is an early work:
Point to the Statue of Liberty,
50″ × 72″, 1979

That is why I enjoy a secret excitement in pursuing these 100 tributes to Our Liberty Lady. A sort of naive passion keeps me constantly venturing and digging into Her immeasurable facets. I regard the Statue of Liberty not merely as a statue, but a friend, a sister, a lady, a woman, a mother, a lover, a fighter, a dreamer, an artist, an actress, a star, a queen, a Goddess, a symbol, a monument, a being living with us every day, every moment, every second. She is in our eyes, mind, consciousness and conscience. I cannot imagine our world without Her: it would be like ideals without words, life without light.

This is why I have painted 100 different paintings of Her, 100 different aspects and situations about our Lady. In one sense, my art is a kind of conceptual art. Neo-Iconography is opening your eyes to see, your imagination to search, your mind to love, and your talent to create a new world for this age of universal culture, where converging races, and societies, bound together by technology and media, create a global village of our planet. In our age, icons stand out from history and culture, and Neo-Iconography becomes more and more evident as one of the most appropriate art forms for creation. For, by centering on icons, we possess the key of "Freedom:" freedom in style, technique, material, combination, situation, encounter.

As this Centennial Celebration of the Statue of Liberty will be a big event in Her history, I hope these 100 bouquets of my humble tribute may become a memorial milestone for Neo-Iconography. ⟩

TSING-FANG CHEN PAINTS THE UNIVERSAL AGE

by Douglas Finlay

Almost instinctively the masters of art, in their work, elicited images and icons as the age demanded, providing a cultural and historical text of time. Whether they be like Rousseau's sleeping gypsy, Picasso's oddly wonderful women, Miro's little beasties, or like Hopper's mornings, Wyeth's children, de Kooning's shark-toothed ladies or Rothko's color fields, they are not so nearly at rest in museums—footnotes to the period—as we might think. Rather, these and other icons by major modern art figures are being given new and vital meaning as they merge with present-day icons and symbols to create an intriguing art form and movement called neo-iconography, initiated by Dr. Tsing-fang Chen.

Chen explains that neo-iconography is expression in painting of the universal age, a convergency of many cultural symbols past and present to create a renaissance of art and history on the canvas. It is a movement Chen has been developing for over 15 years, and to which he has devised a theory, lest the casual observer interpret only mockery in the Mona Lisa wearing sunglasses, the Statue of Liberty reflecting bountifully in both her eyes. More subtle in such a painting is the marriage of both time and space to "create history on the canvas itself" mentioned Chen. Yet, while one notes that a handful of pop artists today juxtapose current-day banal images with historical icons to create comic or serio-comic images—and to which Chen's work admits to a few—they very likely lack the theoretical structures which guide Chen's visions.

Born in Taiwan, Chen was the first Taiwanese to receive a doctorate in art history from the famed Sobonne in Paris, after completing his dissertation on the comparative studies of abstract art and Chinese calligraphy. He also spent seven years at the Ecole Nationale des Beaux-Arts, studying painting. Of Eastern persuasion and upbringing, he began art in earnest at the youthful age of 15, and was soon hungry for anything and everything the masters of western art and literature could feed and nourish him with.

His early drawings were constructed in charcoal, because as he intimated, "with charcoal, one is able to capture the essentials with one color." He maintained that all "qualities of painting lie within charcoal." Continually drawing the same image over, he discovered that "after 100 times I found strength in the stroke, and after 200 times the life would come into the image." This discipline through the years, in part, has enabled him to adapt the many styles and strokes of major art figures, and incoporate them in his works.

While living in Paris, two developments running almost parallel decided which direction his future work would take. On the one hand, he had developed a cultural crisis, where his Eastern values of harmony and passiveness contrasted sharply with his emerging Western values of individualization. On the other, as a learned art historian, he developed a belief that mankind was ultimately guided by two dreams: to reach toward the skies to land on the Moon and planets, and to have peace, "wholeness," among all humanity. In 1969 man landed on the Moon. The event spawned Chen's "The Real Moon," a painting of two astronauts on the Moon watched over by the image of Raphael's "Madonna and the Chair", ca. 1507, set in an orb, as though it were the Earth—as Moon to the Moonmen. This work in watercolor suggested that as man had conquered his first dream, he could now set to his second—conquering the Moon-like Earth not with technology, but with the love depicted by the Madonna with the Christ child. The orb, symbolized the self-fulfillment and harmony of the East. With man's greatest achievement brought about by the West's scientific marvels, he could now look to the centuries-old circle of the East for spirituality and self-fulfillment.

The convergences of images both past and present are essences of neo-iconography. The technique is one of synthesis, the new vision, one of "wholeness." The resolution of Chen's own personal cultural crisis followed.

In discussing the emergence of his work, Chen claimed that "no period in time is better than now because of the richness of icons," icons being, loosely defined, collective subconscious symbols that both identify and perpetuate a cultural people. Chen maintained that the information age has brought the icons and images of the world's cultures into the living room via TV; they are now easily accessible. "We have entered into a universal civilization," said Chen, "in which neo-iconography becomes the most suitable form of expression for the age."

In his current Statue of Liberty series being unveiled in groups over time, Chagall's green fiddler dances atop the Lady of Freedom's pointed crown; Van Gogh's starry nights are visited by the Lady: the blue background of Hopper's Sunday morning is pierced by the image of the stately lady. Chen displays formidable talent at reproducing the styles of the masters. Chagall's fauve colors are there; Van Gogh's intense pulsating strokes are wholly believable; Seurat's luminating pointalism is near picture perfect. Though criticised by some as only good representations of the originals, he feels they recognize only the secondary qualities of the work, and miss the message of the painting.

Pop art, defined by its current-day figurative icons, is the precursor to neo-iconography, asserted Chen. "It is recognizable because it is everyone's property." It is also more social and commercial in context. Not only is Chen able to enrich "everyone's property" with his work, but more: it is one of "continuing the master's works, a 1980's version, adding today's icons, bringing history to the present, renewing history," he concludes.

In developing his school, Chen noted that all important ones take time. "What is at present a phenomenon— universal civilization—will soon become a trend. The consciousness of the public still dates to before 1969, is still involved with divergence."

The present Statue of Liberty series, done in oil, acrylic and charcoal, involves one icon and draws upon techniques and images of major art figures such as Matisse, Picasso, Cezanne, Klee, Gericault, De Chirico, Mondrian, de Kooning, Seurat, and a wealth of others. The point of the series is to "show the diversity of one icon, and to fit in with the masters of the past." ι

—from "SunStorm," April 1986
Douglas Finlay is an editor-writer who profiles artists and critiques art. He has also written extensively about electronics and home furnishings.

BRIEF BIOGRAPHY OF T.F. CHEN
born 1936, Taiwan (Formosa)

Education and Experience
1959: B.A., National Taiwan University, Dept. of Foreign Language and Literature. President of University Association of Fine Arts, 1956–1958.

1961: 13-month worldwide tour and conferences for Moral Rearmament in Japan, India, Switzerland, West Germany, Denmark, Norway, and the United States.

1963: Awarded a scholarship by the French Government to study in Paris.

1964–65: At IPFE, la Sorbonne, obtained two certificates in French language and a diploma (M.A.) in French Contemporary Literature with "honorable mention."

1965–70: At L'Ecole Nationale Superieure des Beaux-Arts, Paris, Atelier Legeult, later Yankel.

1965–70: At la Sorbonne, doctoral thesis on "Chinese Calligraphy and Contemporary Painting" (697 pages), accepted with "very honorable mention," awarded Ph.D. in 1970.
Initiated "Neo-Iconography" in theory and painting.

1970: Tour of important American museums, covering East Coast to Kansas.

1970–75: Intensive trips in Europe, North America, and Japan for cultural exchanges, published numerous articles on art and philosophy.

1975: Nov. moved to USA, lived and painted in New York City.

1977–80: Moved to Maryland, painting, exhibiting, and lecturing.

1980–84: Residence in Washington, D.C., permanent display at Gallery New World. Intensive participation in international art shows, frequent reviews of "Neo-Iconography" in art magazine, newspapers, television.
Attended international cultural conferences such as ICUS in 1980, 1981, 1983, lecturing and joining panel discussions.

1983: Sept. became American citizen
Nov. received "Achievement Award in Arts and Humanities" of Taiwanese-American Foundation."

1984: June, moved to SoHo area, New York City, permanent display at Lucia Gallery, showing in series of "Neo-Iconography."
Nov. returned to Taiwan for extensive exhibitions and lectures.

1985–86: Concentrated on creating 100 paintings for the centennial celebration of "Statue of Liberty" and publishing "The Spirit of Liberty."

Publications
Circulating Corridor, Taipei, 1968, Baffalo Publishing Co.
Notes on Paintings in Paris, Taipei, 1969, Ta Kiang.
Le Petit Prince, translated, 1969, Taipei, Ta Kiang.
Ten Years of My Pictorial Voyages, Taipei, 1974, Lion Art.
"Toward a Universal Approach—Is East-West Convergency at Hand?" (lecture published in English, 1981, and in Japanese, 1982, International Cultural Foundation, Inc.)
The Spirit of Liberty, 1986, Lucia Gallery.

Exhibition and Collection
Besides numerous group shows, more than 50 one-man shows in Asia, Europe, and the United States, including National Historical Museum, Taiwan, 1969, Maison Nationale des Beaux-Arts, Paris, 1971, Art Alliance, Philadelphia, Pa., 1978, New England Center for Contemporary Art, Conn. 1983, lectures and exhibits at Washington Univ., Penn State Univ., Maryland College of Arts and Design, Johns Hopkins Univ. School of Medicine (100 paintings of Neo-iconography for two months, 1981) etc.

More than 1,000 artworks in private collections and museums and institutions such as Museum of Modern Art, Paris; Smithsonian Institution, the White House, etc.

Reviews, Articles, and Information
Besides almost all Chinese newspapers and art magazines in Taiwan, New York, and L.A., etc., reviews, articles, and information on T.F. Chen in *New York Times, Newsweek, New York Magazine, Artnews, Art in America, Art Magazine, Sunstorm, Gallery Guide, The Washington Guide, The Georgetowner, The Uptown Citizen, The Northwest Current, The Asia Mail, Decor, Art Business News, Asia Economic, France-Amerique, Boblingen Zeitung,* etc.

Radio and TV
WHWK-FM (Global Broadcasting), WRKS-FM, WPIX-FM, ELS (Wide World), Cable News Network; NBC, ABC, CBS, Channel 14 D.C., etc.

Video
The Neo-Iconography of T.F. Chen by Van Gogh Video, 1981
East + West = ? by Tularco Enterprises, 1983
Passage to the Fifth Dimension by Tularco Enterprises, 1986

Dr. Tsing-fang Chen with Presidential candidate Walter Mondale, 1984, Los Angeles

Tsing-fang and Lucia Chen with Congressman Stephen Solarz and Mme Solarz, 1984, D.C.

T.F. Chen with Senator Edward Kennedy, 1980, L.A.

Chen at the 9th ICUS where he gave a speech: "Toward a Universal Approach: Is East-West Convergency at Hand?," Miami, 1980

Chen receiving "Achievement Award" in Arts and Humanities of The Taiwanese-American Foundation, Nov. 1983, L.A.

Chen visiting Mark Tobey in Basel, Switzerland, 1971

The Chens with Milton Esterow, editor and publisher of *Artnews,* April 1985

Chen visiting an ancient temple in Seoul, S. Korea, while participating in an international conference there, 1981, summer

Lucia Chen with part of the Chens' collection of African art, May, 1986

John Finger, Lucia Chen, Ms. Dede Bager, and Allen Finger (Executive Director of National Americana Museum) at Lucia Gallery, May, 1986

Introduced by Sir L. Conner, Joe Franklin presents Chen at a Beaux Arts Society Festival, May, 1986

The Chens with Kathy, Mary and Paul Lee.

Chen's family appreciating cherry blossoms at Tidal Basin, Wash., D.C., 1980

As a student at la Sorbonne and L'Ecole des Beaux Arts, T.F. Chen at the Jardin du Luxembourg, Paris, 1968

Outdoor sketching, New Port Beach, L.A., 1981

Chen taking a souvenir pose in Acapulco, Mexico, where he joined an international convention, July, 1981

Chen lecturing on Neo-Iconography, Taiwan, Nov. 1984

Chen's exhibition "100 Paintings" at Johns Hopkins Medical Institute: January-February, 1981

Chen giving a speech for the opening of his show in Taiwan, Nov. 1984

Returning to their homeland, the Chens with Lucia's parents, Chia-yi, 1984

Surrounded by family members and relatives, Tainan, 1984

During an art show in Taipei, Chen chatting with President Chang of Tangchiang Univ. and Mr. Wang, a Taipei City Councilman

The Chens at Lucia Gallery, 90 West Houston St.(SoHo), NYC

The Chens with teachers and good friends of earlier days, after 21 years of separation

The Chens in front of their residence in Silver Spring, Maryland, Dec. 1979

On the day of becoming an American citizen, Chen with son Ted and daughter Julie, Sept. 1983

ACKNOWLEDGMENTS

One day last spring, 1985, my children, Ted and Julie came home from school and emptied out their savings for the restoration of the Statue of Liberty, for Her Centennial Celebration. That was the moment I got the idea to paint 100 paintings of this universal "Icon" for the occasion. So chronologically. I'd like to thank my children together with their school, St. Anthony's. For without the incident, I might never have started these 100 tributes for commemoration.

Through about one year of exciting "producing," both the series and this book, my gratitude to so many friends is enormous. First, to the Honorable Congressman, Mr. Stephen J. Solarz, one of the internationally applauded fighters for Freedom, to whom not only goes my admiration for his achievement in preserving and promoting what Our Liberty Lady stands for, but also my thanks for his encouragement in writing the first page of this book.

Next, to President Reagan, for the honor of quoting his "Eulogy on the Occasion of the Memorial Ceremony of Challenger" (January 31st, 1986, at NASA Center, Houston), for my painting: "Challenging Free Frontiers." (I still bear in mind the deep emotion I experienced by watching TV that day.)

To my dear friend Lawrence Jeppson, once more I would like to express my deep gratitude for his marvelous articles in this book. With vision, he flashed the term "Neo-Iconography" ten years ago, and has been, in one sense, the Godfather of this new art style/school. To Mr. Paul J. Kinney, Museum curator of Liberty Lady, not only do I cherish the happy memory of meeting him during a show of my "Liberty" works, but also I am grateful to him for his opinion of them in writing. Also my thanks go to Mr. Douglas Finlay for his article in *Sunstorm* and for allowing me to put it in this book.

I am deeply grateful to the Honorable Sir Leonard Conner, "World Poet Laureate," for his great contribution in allowing his "official poem" on the Statue of Liberty to appear in this book. Indeed, the eloquence, elegance and excellence of his poem match this rarest occasion of the century. My thanks also go to Ms. Priscella Bain-Smith, for her admirable short comments on many works in this series. They are to my works, fragrance to flowers. I want to thank also Mr. Jong-teh Lin, Mr. Edward Patrick McCue, Ms. Louise Sanders, and Miss Kathy Lee, for their poems which enriched the presentation of these 100 paintings. My gratitude also goes to Dr. Jong Sesin

for his masterful calligraphy (p. 7) which reminds readers of the "parfum" of Oriental culture.

I would like to express my admiration and thanks to Mr. Allen Finger, executive director of the National Americana Museum, together with Ms. Dede Bager of Herald Center; to Mr. Joe Franklin (WOR- Radio & TV), Mr. Hoff (Cable News Network, Inc.), Mr Josef Kaufman (German TV), Mr. Richard Roffman (ELA, WHWK-FM), and Mr. Bill Bertenshaw (WRKS-FM, WPIX-FM), all TV/Radio producers; to Mr. Geno Rodriguez of Alternative Museum, Mr. Karino and Mr. Mano of the Nippon Club; to Mr. Dan Warner of Art Network; to Mr. Gosfield and Ms. Siskrind of *New York Magazine,* to Mr. and Mrs. Forbes of *Sunstorm,* to Ms. Joan Shephard of *The Daily News, NY,* to Mr. Goldstein, Mr. Bendewald of the Statue of Liberty Gallery; and to Mr. Warren Richmond, Mr. Charles Mingus III, Mr. Guy Gigleo and Mr. Jay Gallagher, etc. for their hearty encouragement, valuable arrangements, and meaningful cooperation.

Determined to publish this book by myself with only a few months left before July 4th this year, the official centennial birthday of the Statue of Liberty, my special thanks are due to Mr. and Mrs. Paul and Mary Lee, Dr. and Mrs. Michael Shiau, Dr. and Mrs. Tseu-shong and May-sing Yang, Mme Frances Pecker, Mme Carol Dawn, Prof. and Mrs. Ching-lai Hwang, Dr. and Mrs. Ming-liang Lee, Prof. and Mrs. Joseph C.C. Kuo, Mr. and Mrs. Stephen Hwang, Dr. and Mrs. Fu-tong Shu, and Dr. and Mrs. Rong-san Yu, etc. Their patronage, support, and care facilitated the publication of this book.

Because of extremely tight deadlines imposed for the preparation of this book, I owe special appreciation to Mr. Ken Showell, photographer; to Ms. Patricia Mock and Mr. Michael Markham, of Creative Zone; to Mr. Herb Kelman, Mr. Dan Kelman, and Mr. Wallach of Preferred Press Inc., etc. Without their laudable cooperation, this book might not have been able to come out in time.

Finally my warmest admiration goes to my beloved wife, Lucia. She saw the birth, pain, labor, excitement of this series of paintings and this book from the beginning to the end, and shared with me the hard work every day, every hour and in all situations. Her assistance and tenacity make it fair for me to say that these 100 paintings together with this book are humble tributes from both of us to Our Liberty Lady on Her Centennial Celebration.

T.F. Chen, 5/V/86

LIST OF ART WORKS
COLOR PLATES

IN BLACK AND WHITE